Health and Safety 101

Principles of Health and Safety leadership and engagement

Darren Preston

Health and Safety programming

Darren Preston

Published by Darren Preston, 2023.

While every precaution has been taken in the preparation of this book, the publisher assumes no responsibility for errors or omissions, or for damages resulting from the use of the information contained herein.

HEALTH AND SAFETY PROGRAMMING

First edition. November 30, 2023.

Copyright © 2023 Darren Preston.

ISBN: 979-8223435518

Written by Darren Preston.

Foreword

Establishing a Health and Safety program in the workplace is one of the most effective ways of protecting our most valuable asset, our employees. Losing workers to injury or illness, even for a short time, can cause significant disruption and cost to the business as well as the individual and their families. It can also damage workplace morale, productivity, turnover, and reputation. Health and Safety programs foster a proactive approach to "finding and fixing" site specific hazards before they can escalate into injury or illness. Rather than reacting to an incident, leadership teams and colleagues, collaborate to identify and solve issues before they occur. This collaboration builds trust, enhances communication, provides a safe working environment, and often leads to other business improvements.

Safety in the workplace is not only an organizational requirement and obligation, but also an individual's responsibility. Although legislation varies from country to country, the process is the same with standards being very similar and there are many people that look at this from a moral standpoint. The core functions of these legislations no matter what country you are in are:

1. To take reasonable care for the Health and Safety of themselves and other persons who may be affected by their acts or omissions.
2. To co-operate with their Employer (and other persons) to enable any statutory duty to be performed or complied with.
3. Employees are responsible for acting in a way that does not put themselves or others at risk.
4. To help simplify and condense systems and processes in order to achieve measurable goals.
5. Ensure that everyone goes home safe and well every single day.

Introduction

An effective Health and Safety program emphasizes leadership ownership, participation by employees, and a "find and fix" approach to workplace hazards. The "find and fix" approach to workplace hazards refers to the "Hazard Identification" and Hazard Prevention and Control. Because of the wide variety of different industry conditions, these two core elements should be implemented on a site-specific, industry specific basis in order to effectively detect and correct hazards.

The concept of continuous improvement is key to these recommended Health and Safety practices. As with any journey, long or short, the first step is often the most challenging. The idea is to begin with a simplistic program and grow from that point and over time. By initially focusing on achieving small modest goals, monitoring performance, and evaluating outcomes, the business progresses along a path to higher levels of Health and Safety.

The benefits of effective programmes:

We know as leaders or as a leadership team, that the main goal of a Health and Safety program is to prevent work-related injuries, illnesses, and deaths, as well as the suffering and financial hardship these events can cause workers, their families, and their employers.

Employers may find that implementing these safe practices, simple or complex, bring other benefits as well. The renewed or enhanced commitment to Health and Safety and the cooperative commitment between employers and employees have been linked to:

- Improvements in productivity and quality.
- Better employee morale.
- Improved employee recruitment and retention.
- A more favourable image and reputation (among customers, suppliers, and the community and the internal workforce).

HEALTH AND SAFETY PROGRAMMING

10 steps to safety:

There are 10 simple steps we should consider when implementing a sustainable, engaging, and robust Health and Safety programme. Completing these steps gives us a solid base from which to take on some of the more structured and complex actions needed during the continuous management of safe working practices.

1. Establish Health and Safety as a core value. At every opportunity, we must make sure our colleagues know that finishing the day and going home safely is the way we do business. Assure them that we will work with them to find and fix any hazards that could put them at risk of injury.

2. Lead by example. Practice safe behaviours as leaders and make safety part of our daily conversations with Employees. To gain and sustain successful employee engagement, leadership teams must be seen to set examples and embrace safety as a core value.

3. Implement a reporting system. Develop and communicate a simple reporting system for workers to report any injuries, incidents (including near misses/good catch), hazards, or other Health and Safety concerns, without fear of retaliation. Include an option for reporting anonymously. It should be encouraged to make reports and respect those who do wish to remain anonymous.

4. Provide training. It is a key that we provide training to Employees on how to identify and control hazards in the workplace, as well as report injuries, illnesses, and near misses.

5. Conduct inspections. Inspect the workplace and where possible do this with workers and ask them to identify any activity, piece of equipment, or materials that concern them. Use checklists to help identify problems. Checklists also provide an audit trail.

6. Collect and celebrate ideas. Ask colleagues for ideas on improvements and follow up on their suggestions. Provide them with updates as to help them feel appreciated.

7. Implement hazard controls. Process actions accordingly by implementing and evaluating the solutions available and reasonably practicable. An action tracker is a key tool for finding trends.

8. Address emergencies. Identify foreseeable emergency scenarios and develop instructions on what to do in each. Communicate these procedures and post them in a visible location in the workplace.

9. Seek input on workplace changes. Before making significant changes to the workplace, work organization, equipment, or materials, consult with key team members to identify potential safety or health issues.

10. Make improvements. Set aside a regular time to discuss Health and Safety issues, with the goal of identifying ways to improve the program.

To ensure a solid base is formed, all steps must come together. Just one missing piece will create inconsistencies, and all efforts would become strained. As a leadership team we must find a balance and give each step, equal attention.

Core elements

Core elements are the foundations for safe working practices and a sustainable safety programme. In essence, safety is in itself an overarching core value that should be considered during every decision, process, or program withing our business. Management meeting should hold Health and Safety at the highest regard.

Core elements are used to integrate Health and Safety as a core value withing our business. In doing so, it represents Leadership commitment and ownership. Although Core elements themselves are not a legal requirement, depending on the country, they are a necessity for compliance. There are 6 Core elements:

1, leadership

Leadership teams demonstrate their commitment to eliminating hazards and to continuously improving workplace safety, communicates that commitment to workers, and sets expectations and responsibilities. Leadership means that managers, and supervisors:

O Make Employee safety a core organizational value.

O Are fully committed to eliminating hazards, protecting employees, and continuously improving workplace safety.

O Provide sufficient resources to implement and maintain the Health and Safety program (the right tools for the job).

O Visibly demonstrate and communicate their Health and Safety commitment to employees and others.

O Set an example through their own actions.

Action item 1: Communicate your commitment to Health and Safety.
A clear, written policy helps you communicate that Health and Safety is a primary organizational value and–as important as productivity, profitability, product or service quality, and customer satisfaction.

How to accomplish it
Establish a written policy signed by management describing the organization's commitment to Health and Safety and pledging to establish and maintain a program for all colleagues.

O Communicate the policy to all Employees and, at appropriate times and places, to relevant parties, including:

o Contractors, subcontractors, staffing agencies, and temporary workers on site.

o Suppliers and vendors.

o Visitors.

o Customers.

O Reinforce management commitment by considering Health and Safety in all business decisions, including contractor and vendor selection, purchasing, and facility design and modification. Vendor selection is a key element to the process as it is desired that they hold similar values.

O Be visible in operations and set an example by following the same safety procedures you expect Colleagues to follow. Begin work meetings with a discussion or review of Health and Safety indicators and any outstanding safety items if required. Not much time has to be allocated to this discussion but, it is important to ensure consistent monitoring.

Action item 2: Define goals.

By establishing specific goals and objectives, it sets expectations for managers, supervisors, and employees and for the program overall. The goals and objectives should focus on specific actions that will improve workplace safety. Goals can be both long and short term, simplistic or complex. Each industry will have its own priorities.

How to accomplish it

○ We establish realistic, measurable goals for improving Health and Safety operational goals emphasizing injury and illness prevention should be included rather than focusing on injury and illness rates. Condense and simplify these goals in order to ensure all colleagues, no matter the level of education, can participate with full understanding.

○ Continuously develop plans to achieve the goals by assigning tasks, actions, and responsibilities to particular people, setting timeframes, and determining resource needs.

Action item 3: Allocate resources.

Leaders need to provide the resources needed to implement the Health and Safety program, pursue program goals, and address program shortcomings when they are identified. Although in most facilities there is a dedicated EHS position to Manage this, all leadership teams have a certain amount of responsibility and indeed accountability.

How to accomplish it

O Estimate the resources needed to establish and implement the program or current projects.

O Allow time, when possible, for colleagues to participate in the process.

O Integrate EHS into planning and budgeting processes.

O Provide and direct resources to operate and maintain the program, in order to meet EHS commitments, and pursue goals.

Action item 4: Performance.

Leadership teams lead the program effort by establishing roles and responsibilities and providing an open, positive environment that encourages communication about Health and Safety. Most accountability sits with EHS managers but, Senior leaders also have responsibilities that they need to fulfil.

How to accomplish it

O A business Identifies a person or persons to lead the safety program effort, make plans, coordinate activities, and track progress. Define and regularly communicate responsibilities and who implements and maintains the program and hold people accountable for performance.

HEALTH AND SAFETY PROGRAMMING

O Provide positive recognition for meeting or exceeding Health and Safety goals aimed at preventing injury and illness (e.g., reporting near misses, attending training, conducting inspections).

O We establish ways for leadership teams and colleagues to communicate freely and often about Health and Safety issues without fear of retaliation.

2, Worker Participation

To be effective, any Health and Safety program needs the participation of all employees and their safety representatives. Employees have much to gain from a successful program and the most to lose if it fails. They also often know the most about potential hazards associated with their jobs. Leaders should tap into this knowledge base at every opportunity. Those who do the job, know the risks.

Colleague participation means that they are involved in establishing, operating, evaluating, and improving the Health and Safety program. All colleagues should, at the very least, be given the opportunity to participate,

To have an effective program, all workers:

○ Are encouraged to participate and feel comfortable providing input and reporting Health and Safety concerns.

○ Require access to information they need to participate effectively.

○ Are given opportunities to participate in all stages of program design and implementation. If possible, having safety representatives is a key consideration.

○ Do not experience retaliation when they raise concerns, report injuries, illnesses, and hazards.

Worker participation is vital to the success of Health and Safety programs. To ensure we take all opportunities presented, we look to create actions for our leadership teams.

HEALTH AND SAFETY PROGRAMMING

Action item 1: Encourage workers participate in the program.

By encouraging workers to participate in the program, management signals that it values their input into Health and Safety decisions.

How to accomplish it

○ Give employees the necessary time and resources to participate in the program.

○ Acknowledge and provide positive reinforcement to those who participate in the program and of course, encourage those who don't.

○ Maintain an open-door policy that invites workers to talk to leaders about Health and Safety and to make suggestions.

Action item 2: Encourage Employees to report Health and Safety concerns.

Shop floor colleagues are ideally positioned to identify Health and Safety concerns and shortcomings, such as workplace hazards, unsafe conditions, near misses, and actual incidents. By encouraging reporting and following up promptly on all reports, employers can address issues before someone gets hurt or becomes ill.

How to accomplish it

○ Establish a process for workers to report injuries, illnesses, near misses, hazards, and other Health and Safety concerns, and respond to reports promptly. We must endeavour to include an option for anonymous reporting to reduce fear of reprisal.

○ Ensure we report back to workers routinely and frequently about action taken in response to their concerns and suggestions.

O Emphasize that the leadership team will use reported information only to improve workplace Health and Safety and that no worker will experience retaliation for bringing concerns forward.

O Empower all workers to initiate or request a temporary suspension or shut down of any work activity or operation they believe to be unsafe. We call this the stop work authority which should upheld at senior leadership level.

O Involve workers in finding solutions to reported issues.

Action item 3: Give workers access to information.
Sharing relevant Health and Safety information with colleagues fosters trust and helps organizations make more informed decisions.
How to accomplish it

O Ensure to give employees the information they need to understand Health and Safety hazards and control measures in the workplace. Some Health and Safety regulations require employers to make specific types of information available to workers, such as:

o Material Safety Data Sheets (MSDS)

o Injury and illness communications

o Results of environmental exposure monitoring conducted in the workplace (prevent disclosure of personal information)

o Risk assessments

o COSHH assessments

O Other useful information employees can review include:

o Chemical and equipment manufacturer safety recommendations

o Workplace inspection reports

o Incident investigation reports

o Workplace job hazard analyses such as ergonomic assessments.

Action item 4: Involve employees in all aspects of the program when possible.

Including employee or employee safety representatives' input at every step of the programmes design and implementation improves our ability to identify the presence and causes of workplace hazards. It creates a sense of ownership among staff, enhances their understanding of how the program works, and helps sustain the program over time.

How to accomplish it

Provide opportunities for workers to participate in all aspects of the program, including, but not limited to helping:

O Develop the program and set goals.

O Report hazards and develop solutions that improve Health and Safety.

O Analyse hazards in each step of routine and nonroutine jobs, tasks, and processes.

O Define and document safe work practices.

O Conduct plant inspections.

O Develop and revise safety procedures and policies.

O Participate in incident and accident/near miss investigations.

O Train new employees.

O Develop, implement, and evaluate training programs.

O Evaluate Health and Safety performance and identify ways to improve it.

○ Take part in exposure monitoring and medical surveillance associated with health hazards.

Action item 5: Remove barriers to participation.

To participate meaningfully in the program, workers must feel that their input is welcome, their voices will be heard, and they can access reporting mechanisms. Participation will be suppressed if language, education, or skill levels in the workplace are not considered, or if workers fear retaliation or discrimination for speaking up. For example, if investigations focus on blaming individuals rather than the underlying conditions that led to the incident or if reporting an incident or concern could jeopardize the integrity of workplace relationships.

How to accomplish it

O Ensure that workers from all levels of the business can participate regardless of their skill level, education, or language.

O Provide frequent and regular feedback to show employees that their Health and Safety concerns are being heard and addressed.

O Arrange sufficient time and resources to facilitate participation; for example, hold Health and Safety meetings during regular working hours.

O Ensure that the program protects colleagues from retaliation when reporting injuries, illnesses, and hazards, participating in the program. We must always ensure that other policies do not discourage worker participation.

**THE RELATIONSHIP FACTOR IN
SAFETY LEADERSHIP:**
ACHIEVING SUCCESS THROUGH EMPLOYEE ENGAGEMENT

HEALTH AND SAFETY PROGRAMMING

One of the root causes of workplace injuries, illnesses, and incidents is the failure to identify or recognize hazards that are present, or that could have been anticipated. A critical element of any effective Health and Safety program is a proactive, ongoing process to identify and assess such hazards.

Hazard identification is the first step in the five steps to risk assessments, and it is one of the most important steps. Hazards are the root cause of Health and Safety risks, so it's impossible to keep workplaces safe without identifying them. Risk assessments will be carried out based on the hazards that are identified.

3, Hazard identification and assessment

To identify and assess hazards, leaders Health and Safety professionals, and were applicable, employees:

O Collect and review information about the hazards present or likely to be present in the workplace.

O Conduct initial and periodic workplace inspections of the workplace to identify new or recurring hazards.

O Investigate injuries, illnesses, incidents, and near misses to determine the underlying hazards, their causes, and Health and Safety program shortcomings.

O Group similar incidents and identify trends in injuries, illnesses, and hazards reported.

O Consider hazards associated with emergency or nonroutine situations.

O Determine the severity and likelihood of incidents that could result for each hazard identified and use this information to prioritize corrective actions.

Some hazards, such as housekeeping, can and should be fixed as they are found. Fixing hazards on the spot emphasizes the importance of Health and Safety and takes advantage of a safety leadership opportunity. The leadership team should always be on the lookout for hazards during daily activities, no matter the location, office, factory, or warehouse.

Some reduction methods are a quick fix and can be rectified promptly but there are others that require planning and can become time consuming. This is a great opportunity to involve various members of the leadership team and shop floor colleagues.

For hazard identification and assessment, we set ourselves 5 actions. These are predominantly managed by Health and Safety professionals, but all leaders must participate in the process.

Action item 1: Collect existing information about workplace hazards.
Information on workplace hazards may already be available to leaders and colleagues, from both internal and external sources.

How to accomplish it

Collect, organize, and review information with workers to determine what types of hazards may be present and which workers may be exposed or potentially exposed. Information available in the workplace may include:

O Equipment and machinery operating manuals.

O Material Safety Data Sheets (MSDS) provided by chemical manufacturers.

O Self-inspection reports and inspection reports from authorities and consultants.

O Records of previous injuries and illnesses and reports of incident investigations.

O Trends of frequently occurring injuries and illnesses.

O Monitoring of exposure results.

O Existing Health and Safety programs (lockout/tagout, confined spaces, process safety management, personal protective equipment, etc.).

O Input from workers, including surveys or minutes from Health and Safety committee meetings.

O Results of job hazard analyses, also known as job safety analyses.

Action item 2: Inspect the workplace for safety hazards.

Hazards can be introduced over time as workstations and processes change, equipment or tools become worn, maintenance is not to schedule, or housekeeping practices decline. Setting aside time to regularly inspect the workplace for hazards can help identify shortcomings so that they can be addressed before an incident occurs.

How to accomplish it

O Conduct regular inspections of all operations, equipment, work areas and facilities. Have workers participate on the inspection team where possible and talk to them about hazards that they see or report.

O Document inspections so we can later verify that hazardous conditions are corrected. Take photos or video of problem areas to facilitate later discussion and brainstorming about how to control them, and for use as learning aids.

O Include all areas and activities in these inspections, such as storage and warehousing, facility, and equipment maintenance, purchasing and office functions, and the activities of on-site contractors, subcontractors, and temporary employees Departments must take an element of responsibilities for contractors in their areas.

O Regularly inspect plant vehicles (e.g., forklifts) if applicable to the site.

O Use checklists that highlight things to look for. Typical hazards fall into several major categories, such as those listed below; each workplace will have its own list:

o General housekeeping

o Slip, trip, and fall hazards.

o Electrical hazards

o Equipment operation

o Equipment maintenance

o Fire protection

o Work practices

o Ergonomic issues

o Building/property damage

O Before changing operations, workstations, or workflow; making major organizational changes; or introducing new equipment, materials, or processes, we seek the input of colleagues and evaluate the planned changes for potential hazards and related risks. This is a key function regarding change management.

Action item 3: Identify hazards.

Identifying exposure to hazards is typically more complex than identifying physical safety hazards. For example, gases and vapours may be invisible, often have no odour, and may not have an immediate harmful health effect. Health hazards include chemical hazards (solvents, adhesives, paints, toxic dusts, etc.), physical hazards (noise, radiation, heat, etc.), biological hazards (infectious diseases), and ergonomic risk factors (heavy lifting, repetitive motions, vibration). Reviewing workers' medical records, (appropriately redacted to ensure patient/worker privacy) can be useful in identifying health hazards associated with workplace exposures. This is typically done as part of the recruitment process via HR.

How to accomplish it

O Identify chemical hazards —review MSDS and product labels to identify chemicals in your workplace that have low exposure limits, are highly volatile, or are used in large quantities or in unventilated spaces. Identify activities that may result in skin exposure to chemicals.

O Identify physical hazards —identify any exposures to excessive noise (areas where you must raise your voice to be heard by others), elevated heat (indoor and outdoor), or sources of radiation.

O Identify ergonomic risk factors —examine work activities that require heavy lifting, work above shoulder height, repetitive motions, or tasks with significant vibration.

O Conduct quantitative exposure assessments —when possible, using air sampling or direct reading instruments. Typically, we have a specialist company monitor our exposure risks.

Action item 4: Conduct incident investigations

Workplace incidents –including injuries, illnesses, near misses, and reports of other concerns– provide a clear indication of where hazards exist. By thoroughly investigating incidents and reports, will identify hazards that are likely to cause future harm. The purpose of an investigation must always be to identify the root causes (often more than there is more than one route cause) of the incident or concern, in order to prevent re-occurrences.

How to accomplish it

O Develop a clear plan and procedure for conducting incident investigations, so that an investigation can begin immediately when an incident occurs. The plan should cover items such as:

o Who was involved?

o Lines of communication

o Materials, equipment, and supplies

o Reporting forms and templates

O Training of investigative teams on incident investigation techniques.

O Conducting investigations that includes representatives of both management and colleagues.

O Investigate close calls/near misses.

O Identify and analyses of root causes to address underlying program shortcomings that allowed the incidents to happen.

○ Communicate the results of the investigation to managers, supervisors, and colleagues to prevent recurrence.

25

Effective incident investigations do not stop at identifying a single factor that triggered an incident. They ask the questions "Why?" and "What led to the failure?" For example, if a piece of equipment fails, a good investigation asks: "Why did it fail?" "Was it maintained properly?" "Was it beyond its service life?" and "How could this failure have been prevented?" Similarly, a good incident investigation does not stop when it concludes that a colleague made an error. It asks such questions as: "Was the colleague provided with appropriate tools and time to do the work?" "Was the worker adequately trained?" and "Was the worker properly supervised?

Action item 5: Characterize the nature of identified hazards, identify interim control measures, and prioritize the hazards for control.

The next step is to assess and understand the hazards identified and the types of incidents that could result from worker exposure to those hazards. This information can be used to develop interim controls and to prioritize hazards for permanent control.

How to accomplish it

O Evaluate each hazard by considering the severity of potential outcomes, the likelihood that an event or exposure will occur, and the number of workers who might be exposed. This is done and recorded on a risk assessment.

O Use interim control measures to protect workers until more permanent solutions can be implemented.

O Prioritize the hazards so that those presenting the greatest risk are addressed first. however, leadership teams have an ongoing obligation to control all serious recognized hazards and to protect workers.

"Risk" is the product of hazard and exposure. Risk can be reduced by controlling or eliminating the hazard or by reducing employee exposure to hazards. An assessment of risk helps leaders understand hazards in the context of their own workplace and prioritize hazards for permanent control.

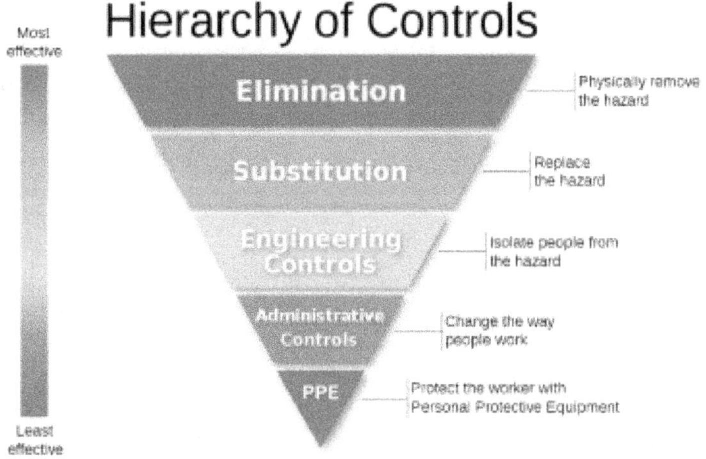

4, Hazard prevention and control

Effective and consistent controls protect colleagues from workplace hazards; help avoid injuries, illnesses, and incidents; minimize or eliminate Health and Safety risks; and help leaders provide colleagues with safe working conditions. We must make every effort as a collective to move away from reactive management and concentrate on a more proactive approach.

To effectively control and prevent hazards, as a leadership team we should:

O Involve employees, who often have the best understanding of the conditions that create hazards and insights into how they can be controlled.

O Identify and evaluate options for controlling hazards, using a "hierarchy of controls."

O Use a hazard control plan to guide the selection and implementation of controls and implement controls according to the plan.

O Develop plans with measures to protect colleagues during emergencies and nonroutine activities.

O Evaluate the effectiveness of existing controls to determine whether they continue to provide protection, or whether different controls may be more effective. Review new technologies for their potential to be more protective, more reliable, or less costly taking into account "reasonably practicable". To do this we set 5 clear actions:

HEALTH AND SAFETY PROGRAMMING

Action item 1: Identify control options.

A wealth of information exists to help leaders investigate options for controlling identified hazards. Before selecting any control options, it is essential to obtain colleague input on their feasibility and effectiveness.

How to accomplish it

Collect, organize, and review information to determine what types of hazards may be present and which workers may be exposed or potentially exposed. Information available in the workplace may include:

O Review sources such as Governmental policy and guidance.

O Investigate control measures used in other workplaces and determine whether they would be effective at your workplace. This is typically done once per month via a global safety call.

O Get input from colleagues who may be able to suggest and evaluate solutions based on their knowledge of the facility, equipment, and work processes. Maintenance team members are a great example. Along with company veterans.

Action item 2: controls

Leaders should select the controls that are the most feasible, effective, and permanent.

How to accomplish it

○ Eliminate or control all serious hazards (hazards that are causing or are likely to cause death or serious physical harm) immediately.

○ Use interim controls while you develop and implement longer-term solutions.

○ Select controls according to a hierarchy that emphasizes engineering solutions (including elimination or substitution) first, followed by safe work practices, administrative controls, and finally personal protective equipment.

○ Avoid selecting controls that may directly or indirectly introduce new hazards.

○ Review control options to ensure that controls are feasible and effective.

○ Use a combination of control options when no single method fully protects workers.

Action item 3: Develop and update risk actions.

A hazard actions matrix describes how the selected controls will be implemented. An effective plan will address serious hazards first. Interim controls may be necessary, but the overall goal is to ensure effective long-term control of hazards. It is important to track progress toward completing the control plan and periodically (at least annually and when conditions, processes or equipment change) verify that controls remain effective. This is also an auditable process during inspections and incident investigations.

How to accomplish it

O List the hazards needing controls in order of priority.

O Assign responsibility for installing or implementing the controls to a specific person or persons with the power or ability to implement the controls.

O Establish a target completion date.

O Plan how to track progress toward completion.

O Plan how to verify the effectiveness of controls after they are installed or implemented.

Action item 4: Implement selected controls in the workplace.

Once hazard prevention and control measures have been identified, they should be implemented according to the hazard control plan.

How to accomplish it

O Implement hazard control measures according to the priorities established in the hazard control plan.

O When resources are limited, implement measures on a "worst-first" basis, according to the hazard ranking priorities (risk) established during hazard identification and assessment. (Regardless of limited resources, Leaders have a legal and moral obligation to protect staff from recognized, serious hazards.)

O Promptly implement any measures that are easy and inexpensive—e.g., general housekeeping, removal of obvious tripping hazards such as electrical cords, basic lighting—regardless of the level of hazard they involve.

Action item 5: Follow up to confirm that controls are effective.

To ensure that control measures are and remain effective, leaders should track progress in implementing controls, inspect and evaluate controls once they are installed, and follow routine preventive maintenance practices.

How to accomplish it

O Track progress and verify implementation by asking the following questions:

o Have all control measures been implemented according to the hazard control plan?

o Have engineering controls been properly installed and tested?

o Have workers been appropriately trained so that they understand the controls, including how to operate engineering controls, safe work practices, and PPE use requirements?

o Are controls being used correctly and consistently?

O Conduct regular inspections.

HEALTH AND SAFETY PROGRAMMING

O Evaluate control measures to determine if they are effective or need to be modified. If controls are not effective, identify, select, and implement further control measures that will provide adequate protection.

O Confirm that work practices, administrative controls, and PPE use policies are being followed.

O Conduct routine preventive maintenance of equipment, facilities, and controls to help prevent incidents due to equipment failure.

5, Education and training

Education and training are important tools for informing leadership teams and colleagues about workplace hazards and controls so they can work more safely and be more productive. Another role of education and training, however, is to provide all employees with a greater understanding of the Health and Safety program itself, so that they can contribute to its development and implementation.

Education and training provide leadership teams and colleagues with:

○ Knowledge and skills needed to do their work safely and avoid creating hazards that could place themselves or others at risk.

○ Awareness and understanding of workplace hazards and how to identify, report, and control them.

○ Specialized training when their work involves unique hazards.

Additional training may be needed depending on the roles assigned to employees for example, managers and supervisors may need specific training to ensure that they can fulfil their roles in providing leadership, direction, and resources for the Health and Safety program. Colleagues assigned specific roles in the program (e.g., Safety champions) may need training to ensure that they are able to fully participate in those roles.

Effective training and education can be provided outside a formal classroom setting. Peer-to-peer training, on-the-job training, and on-site demonstrations can be effective in conveying safety concepts, ensuring understanding of hazards and their controls, and promoting good work practices.

HEALTH AND SAFETY PROGRAMMING

Action item 1: Provide program awareness training.
Managers, supervisors, and workers all need to understand the EHS program's structure, plans, and procedures. Having this knowledge ensures that everyone can fully participate in developing, implementing, and improving the program.

How to accomplish it

○ Provide training to all managers, supervisors, and colleague on:

o Health and Safety policies, goals, and procedures

o Functions of the safety program

o Whom to contact with questions or concerns about the program (including contact information)

o How to report hazards, injuries, illnesses, and near misses

o What to do in an emergency

o The employer's responsibilities in accordance with local legislation.

○ Provide information on the safety hazards of the workplace and the controls for those hazards.

○ Ensure that training is provided in the language(s) and at a literacy level that all workers can understand.

○ Emphasize that the program can only work when everyone is involved and feels comfortable discussing concerns; making suggestions; and reporting injuries, incidents, and hazards.

O Confirm, as part of the training, that all workers have the right to report injuries, incidents, hazards, and concerns and to fully participate in the program without fear of retaliation.

Action item 2: Leadership knowledge.

Leaders are responsible for workers' safety, yet sometimes have little training on safety-related concepts and techniques. They may benefit from specific training that allows them to fulfil their leadership roles in the program.

How to accomplish it

O Reinforce knowledge of their responsibilities under relevant Health and Safety regulations.

O Train leaders on procedures for responding to workers' reports of injuries, illnesses, and incidents, including ways to avoid discouraging reporting.

O Instruct Leadership teams on fundamental concepts and techniques for recognizing hazards and methods of controlling them, including the hierarchy of controls.

O Instruct leadership teams on incident investigation techniques, including root cause analysis.

Action item 3: Train Employees on their specific roles in the Health and Safety program

Additional training may be needed to ensure that workers can incorporate any assigned Health and Safety responsibilities into their daily routines and activities.

How to accomplish it

O Instruct workers on how to report injuries, illnesses, incidents, and concerns.

O Instruct employees on responsibilities within the Health and Safety program and how they should carry out those responsibilities:

o Hazard recognition and controls.

o Participation in incident investigations

o Program evaluation and improvement

O Provide opportunities for employees to ask questions and provide feedback during and after the training.

O As the program evolves, introduce a more formal process for determining the training needs of workers responsible for developing, implementing, and maintaining the program.

Action item 4: Train workers on hazard identification and controls
Providing employees with an understanding of hazard recognition and control and actively involving them in the process can help to eliminate hazards before an incident occurs.
How to accomplish it

O Train Employees on techniques for identifying hazards.

O Train Employees so they understand and can recognize the hazards they may encounter in their own jobs, as well as more general work-related hazards.

O Instruct employees on concepts and techniques for controlling hazards, including the hierarchy of controls and its importance.

HEALTH AND SAFETY PROGRAMMING

○ Train employees on the proper use of work practice and administrative controls.

○ Train employees on when and how to wear required personal protective equipment.

○ Provide additional training, as necessary, when a change in facilities, equipment, processes, materials, or work organization could increase hazards, and whenever a worker is assigned a new task.

"it's better to lose a minute than to lose a life".

40

6, Program evaluation and improvement

Once a Health and Safety program is established, it should be evaluated initially to verify that it is being implemented as intended. After that, leadership teams should periodically, (at least annually), step back and assess what is working and what is not, and whether the program is on track to achieve its goals. Whenever these assessments identify opportunities to improve the program, leadership teams in coordination with employees—should adjust and monitor how well the program performs as a result. Sharing the results of monitoring and evaluation within the workplace, and celebrating successes, will help drive further improvement.

Program evaluation and improvement includes:

O Establishing, reporting, and tracking goals and targets that indicate whether the program is making progress.

O Evaluating the program initially and periodically thereafter to identify shortcomings and opportunities for improvement.

O Providing ways for workers to participate in program evaluation and improvement.

Action item 1: Monitor performance and progress
The first step in monitoring is to define indicators that will help track performance and progress. Next, leadership teams need to establish and follow procedures to collect, analyse, and review performance data.

Both lagging and leading indicators should be used. Lagging indicators generally track worker exposures and injuries that have already occurred. Leading indicators track how well various aspects of the program have been implemented and reflect steps taken to prevent injuries or illnesses before they occur.

How to accomplish it

O Develop and track lagging indicators of progress toward established Health and Safety goals, such as:

o Number and severity of injuries and illnesses

o Results of employee exposure monitoring that show that exposures are hazardous.

O Develop and track leading indicators, such as:

o Level of colleague participation in program activities.

o Number of employee safety suggestions.

o Number of hazards, near misses reported.

o Amount of time taken to respond to reports.

o Number and frequency of management assurance reviews.

o Number and severity of hazards identified during reviews.

o Number of employees who have completed required Health and Safety training.

o Timely completion of corrective actions after a workplace hazard is identified or an incident occurs.

o Timely completion of planned preventive maintenance activities

o Employee opinions about program effectiveness obtained from a safety opinion survey.

HEALTH AND SAFETY PROGRAMMING

O Analyse performance indicators and evaluate progress over time.

O Share results with employees or employee safety representatives and invite their input on how to further improve performance.

O When opportunities arise, share your experience, and compare your results to similar facilities.

Indicators can be either quantitative or qualitative. Whenever possible, select indicators that are measurable (quantitative) and that will help you determine whether you have achieved your program goals. The number of reported hazards and near misses would be a quantitative indicator. A colleague expressing a favourable opinion about program participation would be a qualitative indicator.

Action item 2: Verify that the program is implemented and is operating.

Initially and at least annually, leadership teams need to evaluate the program to ensure that it is operating as intended, is effective in controlling identified hazards, and is making progress toward established Health and Safety goals and objectives. The scope and frequency of program evaluations will vary depending on changes in HSE regulatory changes the complexity, and length of the program; and the types of hazards it must control.

HEALTH AND SAFETY PROGRAMMING

How to accomplish it

O Verify that the core elements of the program have been fully implemented.

O Involve employees where possible in all aspects of program evaluation, including reviewing information such as establishing and tracking performance indicators; and identifying opportunities to improve the program.

O Verify that the following key processes are in place and operating as intended:

o Reporting injuries, illnesses, incidents, hazards, and concerns

o Conducting workplace inspections and incident investigations

o Tracking progress in controlling identified hazards and ensuring that hazard control measures remain effective.

o Collecting and reporting any data needed to monitor progress and performance.

O Review the results of any compliance audits to confirm that any program shortcomings are being identified. Verify that actions are being taken that will prevent recurrence.

Action item 3: Correct program shortcomings and identify opportunities to improve.

Whenever a problem is identified in any part of the Health and Safety program, leadership teams should take prompt action to correct the problem and prevent its recurrence.

How to accomplish it

If you discover program shortcomings, take actions needed to correct them.

O Proactively seek input from managers, workers, supervisors, and other stakeholders on how you can improve the program.

O Determine whether changes in equipment, facilities, materials, key personnel, or work practices trigger any need for changes in the program.

O Determine whether your performance indicators and goals are still relevant and, if not, how you could change them to drive improvements more effectively in workplace Health and Safety.

The scope and frequency of evaluations will depend on the complexity of the program and on the types of hazards it must control. Program evaluations should be conducted periodically (at least annually) but might also be triggered by a change in process or equipment, or an incident such as a serious injury, significant property damage, or an increase in safety-related complaints.

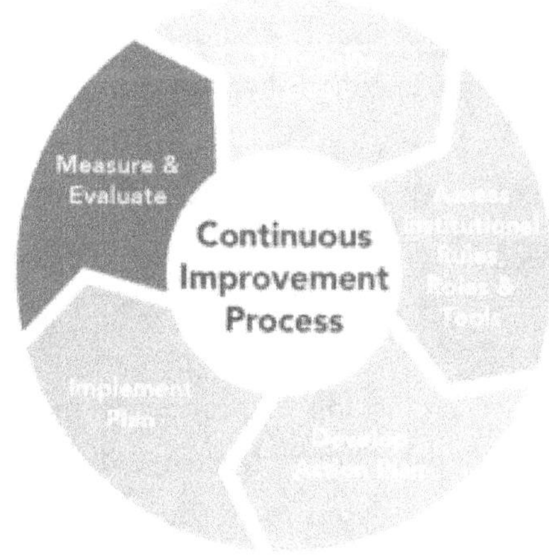

Why don't employees follow the rules?

Getting employees to follow the rules – even those that keep them safe is more difficult than simply having the desire to avoid injuries. Culture, leadership, and other factors make up a complex system that interacts with, influences, and guides workplace behaviour. Aligning these factors is key to developing the behaviour needed to ensure the systems and rules already in place are followed. It's essential to create an adaptable workforce that can recognize risk and respond appropriately. Engagement is the true key to a great culture within any Health and Safety program.

To start building a culture of commitment that runs in conjunction with the Health and Safety program, us as leaders should ask ourselves these questions:

1, What is our real goal?

What is the commitment we are asking employees to make? The real goal is not whether we want to be injury free or reduce injuries. These are important, but they are segregated from the core element of commitment: the view of what safety means to us. How we think about safety, how we see its role in our daily operations, and what defines success – these things shape everything we do and say. As a start, we must consider how we define success. Do we judge safety performance based on the absence of failure? Or do we use a balanced mix of leading and lagging indicators when assessing safety performance? Do we show investment on proactive risk management, or do we wait for prompts?

The scope and frequency of evaluations will depend on the complexity of the program and on the types of hazards it must control. Program evaluations should be conducted periodically (at least annually) but might also be triggered by a change in process or equipment, or an incident such as a serious injury, significant property damage, or an increase in safety-related complaints.

2, Do we understand our culture as it is now?

Culture is an important element of safety success. We have strong, adaptive cultures and tend to have low injury rates. But are we fully aware of the ongoings when leadership is absent from view? Building trust with our colleagues is key to honesty, honesty leads to information. It is important to always remember. As leaders, we need to develop relationships with employees as real people and leaders need to build a culture of commitment – a workplace that supports and encourages engagement.

3, How good is our safety leadership?

Employees cannot change the Safety culture of our plant; that power sits with our leaders. A core set of safety best practices, as well as leadership's transformational style, has a direct relationship to the culture of an organization and its safety results. Once we as leaders understand the strengths and gaps in our safety leadership behaviours, we can reinforce what we're doing well and improve the areas that need help. It's easy to believe others judge our intentions based on our words, but what others see depends on our visual actions and example setting.

support the process.

One key tool we can use to help us on our journey with both building a safety management system and gaining buy in from our colleagues, is to incorporate Safety Champions.

The purpose of a safety champion

A Safety Champion is a position that offers the opportunity to participate in Health and Safety operations on site. It grants the ability to drive safety culture in respective areas and in turn provide feedback to the leadership team. A Champion will be a vocal point for both the leadership team and shop floor colleagues bringing in and helping to implement new ideas and development plans. It is a position of trust which grants a level of ownership and responsibility that will enable an eyes on the ground approach during periods where the leadership team is not available.

Safety champions are people in our workplace that promote safety with their actions. They not only adhere to but also promote and take active roles in safety practices at work. Safety champions can be identified by the following attributes:

◇ Advocating a positive approach to workplace safety

◇ Contributing ideas to help the workplace improve its level of safety.

◇ Promoting the use of safety devices to reduce the risks of injury.

◇ Demonstrating through their day-to-day actions that they genuinely care for the safety and wellbeing of their peers.

◇ Understanding the risks and hazards at work and how to mitigate them.

HEALTH AND SAFETY PROGRAMMING

⬦ Working with management to implement and uphold Health and Safety policies.

The power of safety champions

- *They're safe 24/7*

Safety champions are natural motivators. They know that injuries can happen at any time.

They wear the appropriate PPE consistently, report flawed machinery, and take care whenever they're on site.

These employees regularly participate in workplace training and do their best to share their knowledge with others, improving overall safety awareness. They show concern for their own well-being and the well-being of others.

- *They promote safety training.*

Safety champions know that training is the foundation of success. Safety training helps employees in improving their situational awareness skills and helps decrease the probability of accidents. Safety training provides employees the knowledge they need to prevent accidents in the workplace or in the warehouse.

- *They lead by example.*

Caring for the safety of others and inspiring change is one of the main features of a safety champion. They don't just talk about the importance of safety while applying a different set of rules for themselves. The pride they take in safety inspires others to do the same.

- *They encourage continuous improvement.*

They always look for new methods to improve general safety in the workplace, and they recognize that there is always room for improvement. These kinds of safety measures create continuity and stability, which will lead to more efficient methods to complete simple tasks.

- *They implement action.*

In the case of an emergency, a solid action plan can protect all employees from various potentially dangerous circumstances. Safety leaders create and institute recovery policies that can deal with complex and unforeseen situations. Action plans determine all required processes to intervene if a disaster occurs. These safety champions can be in a position to help leaders with tasks during emergencies.

- *They understand the human factors.*

A person's state of mind significantly influences their attitude towards Health and Safety, and champions will try to understand and address these factors to reduce safety errors. Rushing, frustration, fatigue, and complacency often lead to injuries as much as the hazards themselves, and champions must encourage their co-workers to slow down, and always choose the safest way. For a champion, safety is the most important factor in the workplace.

Who would be a Safety Champion?

It is proposed that there would be 1 Safety Champion per department agreed upon by department heads. This is a voluntary position that must have volunteers in order for the programme to be sustainable.

Accountabilities

A champion will have no accountabilities with full Health and Safety management remaining with the designated manager and/or other leaders. This would be a participation position only for driving Safety values forward. No tasks or legal duties will be given to champions. No extra work is required.

responsibilities

In order for this position to be sustainable, a Champion will need a level of participation. Champions will be key to culture building and the encouragement of safe working practices. The following recommendations are the responsibilities all champions would hold.

HEALTH AND SAFETY PROGRAMMING

- Participate in one Internal champion meeting per month with the designated manager and guest attendees. Agenda provided prior to meeting date.
- Be an additional point of contact for all safety concerns within respective areas. Champions are not to act upon any issues, they are to inform the Health and Safety manager promptly.
- Help drive new processes and support change management though visual support, engagement, and encouragement.
- Bring new ideas forward on behalf of all employees and act as a voice for the shop floor.
- Lead by example though safe working (PPE, reporting incidents, calling it out)
- Join safety walks with the Health and Safety manger and senior leaders (workload dependant)
- Encourage and help motivate employee engagement with Health and Safety.
- Identify risks and hazards through observation and report to the Health and Safety manager for risk reduction analysis.
- Act as an influencer regarding policies and procedures.
- Champion Health and Safety core values
- Help distribute Safety notifications and other materials (workload dependant)

Cost implications

additional salary can or cannot be granted for this voluntary position depending on the company. However, A small level of investment to support and encourage employee development would be Warranted in the form of a Safety awareness course.

Brand your Safety!

Just like a corporate brand, a Health and Safety brand, particularly one which overarches the brands and philosophies of multiple departments, needs to be much more than a logo. It needs to make clear the values, accountabilities and behaviours and it needs to be relevant to all, from leaders to operatives. It should empower and engage all employees, elevating aspirations beyond compliance, enforcement and rule following to a unified, heart-felt belief that they can contribute to doing Health and Safety differently and better.

Design your logo, gain support, source your ambassadors, and strive to be the best, strive to improve and more importantly, ensure everyone goes home safe and well every single day.

To summarise.

The fundamental core value of Health and Safety is to provide a safe place of work with safe access and egress. Suitable provision of relevant information, instruction, training, and supervision. Provide a suitable working environment in regard to also providing suitable arrangements for welfare.

Health and Safety is no easy task but, it can be an exciting and engaging operation that can, if managed correctly, bring out the very best of all employees.

The key questions that involve all employees from the very bottom, to the highest in the company are What, Why, and How.

What is it that we want to do?

Never hide anything from your colleagues. Leaving people out of the discussion in regards to safety can cause serious consequences at a later date. Lack of clarity leads to a lack of trust. Take time to be clear on what it is.

Why are we doing it?

Never hide anything from your colleagues. Sometimes a simple explanation can provide you with a wealth of engagement and participation.

How are we going to do it?

This is the most important part! Never hide anything from your colleagues. As humans we naturally like routine, when we decide to change, it can cause great risk due to the disruption of routine.

What do employees need to know?

What effect will it have on them?

What will be different?

How long will it take to complete the process?

Are there additional duties?

See the words, think the meaning!

"Don't learn safety by accident".
"Respect the unexpected, think through your risks".
"Know safety, no injury. No safety. Know injury".
"Safety comes in a can. I can, you can, we can work safely".
"Safety is a process, processes take time".
"Ear protection is a sound investment".
"Work safe, home safe".
"Standards We Set to Accomplish the Goals We Strive For".
"Safety brings first aid to the uninjured".
"If you don't think it is safe, it probably isn't."
"Carefulness costs you nothing. Carelessness may cost you a life."
"An ounce of prevention is worth a pound of cure."
"Stop! Think! Then Act!"
"Prepare and prevent, don't repair and repent.

THANK YOU!

59

www.ingramcontent.com/pod-product-compliance
Lightning Source LLC
Chambersburg PA
CBHW050613160726
48003CB00003B/1173